1 KNOW BASIC BIBLE TEACHINGS

No one can know all the false teachings of all the cults, but Christians can learn the Bible well enough so that they will recognize cultic doctrine.

Bankers are trained to recognize counterfeit currency by studying genuine dollar bills. Thus, bankers will recognize a counterfeit bill when they come across it. The more a person understands the Bible, the better that person will be able to recognize cultic errors.

Scripture warns about spiritual deception. Galatians 1:8 speaks of "a gospel other than the one we preached to you." Second Corinthians 11:4 warns us to avoid those who preach "[another] Jesus … a different spirit … a different gospel."

Cults often deny or distort three key biblical doctrines:

- The **Trinity**—one God in three Persons
- The person and work of **Jesus Christ**
- The gospel of **salvation** by grace alone through faith

Memorize key apologetic verses and central doctrines:

If a Jehovah's Witness says that the Holy Spirit is a force and not a person, show him or her passages that demonstrate that the Holy Spirit is a person: 1 Corinthians 2:11–12; 12:11; Ephesians 4:30; Romans 8:26-27.

The Trinity:

- **There is only one God**—Isaiah 43:10-11; 44:6,8; 45:21-22; 46:9; John 17:3; 1 John 5:20-21.
- **Father is God**—1 Peter 1:2; Philippians 2:11
- **Son is God**—Matthew 1:23; John 1:1; 20:28; Hebrews 1:8; 2 Peter 1:1; Titus 2:13
- **Holy Spirit is God**—Acts 5:3-4; 1 Corinthians 3:16-17; 2 Corinthians 3:17

The Person of Jesus Christ:

- **He is eternal and uncreated**—Isaiah 9:6; Hebrews 7:3; Micah 5:2; John 1:1-3; 8:58; Colossians 1:15-19
- **He retained his deity while becoming a man**—Philippians 2:5-11; Colossians 1:19; 2:9; Hebrews 1:3-8
- **He is equal in nature to God the Father**—John 5:18; John 19:7
- **He receives the same honor and worship as the Father**—John 5:23; Hebrews 1:6; Revelation 5:11-14; John 14:14

The Gospel of Salvation:

- **Salvation is a free gift**—Romans 6:23; 1 John 5:11-13
- **Salvation is by faith alone apart from works**—Acts 16:30-31; John 5:24; 6:28-29,47; Ephesians 2:8-9; Titus 3:5; Romans 3:28; 4:4-8; 8:1; 11:6; Galatians 3:1-3; Philippians 3:9
- **Works are the natural result of saving faith**—Eph. 2:10; James 2:14

RESOURCES

The inclusion of a work or web site does not necessarily mean the endorsement of all its contents or of other works by the same author(s) or organization.

LITERATURE

General

The Challenge of the Cults and New Religions by Ron Rhodes (Zondervan, 2001)

Correcting the Cults: Expert Responses to Their Scripture Twisting by Norman L. Geisler and Ron Rhodes (Baker, 2005)

Scripture Twisting: Twenty Ways the Cults Misread the Bible by James Sire (InterVarsity, 1980)

A Guide to New Religious Movements by Ronald Enroth, ed. (InterVarsity, 2005)

Cults and the Occult, 4th ed. by Edmond C. Gruss (P&R, 2002)

Charts of Cults, Sects & Religious Movements by H. Wayne House (Zondervan, 2000)

So What's the Difference?: A Look at 20 Worldviews, Faiths and How They Compare to Christianity by Fritz Ridenour (Gospel Light, 2001)

The Unexpected Journey: Conversations with People Who Turned from Other Beliefs to Jesus by Thom S. Rainer (Zondervan, 2005)

Cults in Our Midst by Margaret Thaler Singer with Janja Lalich (Jossey-Bass, 2003)

Recovery from Cults: Help for Victims of Psychological and Spiritual Abuse by Michael Langone, ed. (W.W. Norton, 1993)

Mormonism

Reasoning from the Scriptures with the Mormons by Ron Rhodes and Marian Bodine (Harvest House, 1995)

Speaking the Truth in Love to Mormons by Mark Cares (WELS, 1998)

Where Does It Say That? by Bob Witte (WELS, 1998) www.irr.org/resources.html

Mormonism 101: Examining the Religion of the Latter-day Saints by Bill McKeever and Eric Johnson (Baker, 2000)

Jehovah's Witnesses

Reasoning from the Scriptures with the Jehovah's Witnesses by Ron Rhodes (Harvest House, 1993)

Jehovah's Witnesses Answered Verse by Verse by David A. Reed (Baker, 1986)

Jehovah's Witnesses by Robert M. Bowman, Jr. (Zondervan, 1995)

Other Groups

Mind Sciences by Todd Ehrenborg (Zondervan, 1995)

"Jesus Only" Churches by E. Calvin Beisner (Zondervan, 1995)

New Age Movement by Ron Rhodes (Zondervan, 1995)

POWERPOINT®

Christianity, Cults and Religions (Rose Publishing, 2006)

10 Questions and Answers on Mormonism (Rose Publishing, 2007)

10 Questions and Answers on Jehovah's Witnesses (Rose Publishing, 2007)

Denominations Comparison (Rose Publishing, 2005)

Why Trust the Bible? (Rose Publishing, 2007)

10 Keys to Witnessing to Cults (Rose Publishing, 2008)

INTERNET

Reasoning from the Scriptures Ministries www.RonRhodes.orgs

Witnesses for Jesus, Inc.   www.4witness.org

Watchman Fellowship   www.watchman.org

Personal Freedom Outreach   www.pfo.org

Evidence Ministries   www.evidenceministries.org

Mormons in Transition   www.irr.org/mit

Mormonism Research Ministry   www.mrm.org

TowerWatch Ministries   www.towerwatch.com

VIDEO/DVD

The Witness at Your Door and *The Witness Goes Out!* (Jeremiah Films, 1992)

In the Name of Jehovah (North American Mission Board, 2004)

Speaking the Truth in Love to Mormons (WELS media, n.d.) www.truthinloveministry.net/material.htm

The Mormon Puzzle (North American Mission Board, 1997)

The Bible vs. the Book of Mormon (Living Hope Ministries, 2005)

WHAT IS A CULT?

DEFINITIONS

As cult expert Alan Gomes has stated, "cults grow out of and deviate from a previously established religion."

Therefore, a cult of Christianity would be a group of people that claim to be Christian yet hold to "a particular doctrinal system" set forth by a leader, group of leaders, or organization which "denies … one or more of the central doctrines of the Christian faith."
(Ron Rhodes, *The Challenge of the Cults and New Religions*; Grand Rapids, MI: Zondervan, 2001)

Christianity's central doctrines include:

- God (Trinity)
- The deity and work of Jesus Christ on the cross
- Humanity's sinfulness
- Salvation by grace alone through faith
- The authority of Scripture

Cults of Christianity are groups whose claims about these central doctrines contradict what the Bible teaches including …

> Jehovah's Witnesses
> Mormonism
> Christian Science
> The Family/Children of God
> Unification Church
> Christadelphians
> Oneness Pentecostalism

but excluding other groups such as …

> **Scientology** (no direct relation to a previously established religion, despite the cross in their logo)
> **Hare Krishna** (no biblical basis claimed; little reference to Jesus)

Three main types of injury from false beliefs:

Physical—In some cases, followers of Christian Science have died because they rejected medical treatment, believing that sickness and death are illusions. Jehovah's Witnesses have lost their lives because they refused blood transfusions, believing the cult's teaching that receiving a blood transfusion violates Jehovah's law. In these and other groups, people have unwittingly believed something and lost.

Emotional—Members of a cult often feel extreme guilt because they're trapped in a system in which they have to earn their salvation—the standards being so high that they can never completely measure up. They are required to obey the cult's rules precisely, and if they fail, they're not saved.

Spiritual—Cults proclaim a different Jesus by denying what the Bible teaches about who Jesus is and what he did for us on the cross. Thus, they redefine the gospel of salvation. If people have a counterfeit Jesus with a counterfeit gospel, then they have a counterfeit salvation.

To witness effectively, you need a strategy. Following these key points will greatly increase your success when cultists show up on your doorstep.

Share the Truth with Respect

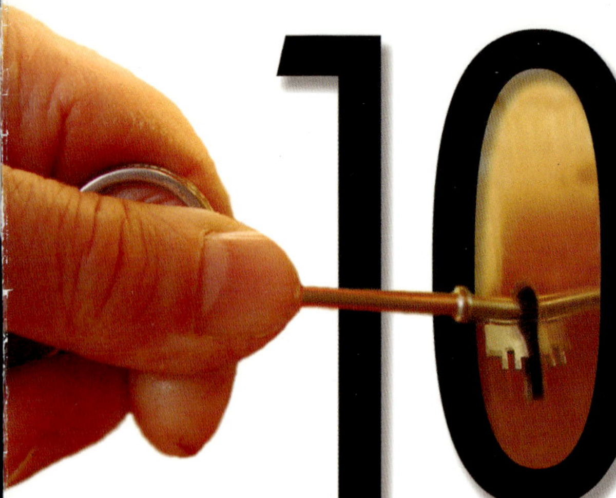

10 keys to WITNESSING to cults

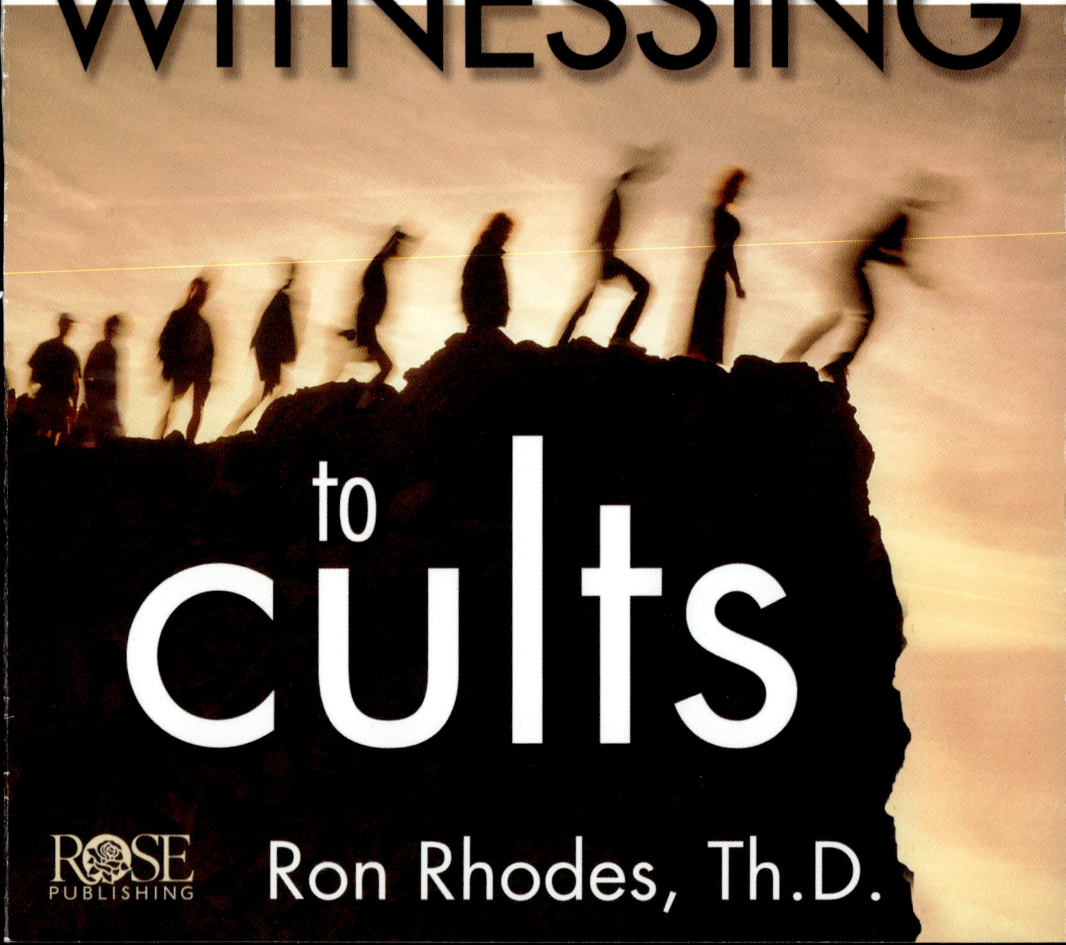

ROSE PUBLISHING

Ron Rhodes, Th.D.

10 GIVE YOUR TESTIMONY

Cultists need to hear what God has done in your life.

You might not be an expert in theology, the Bible, cultic doctrines, or apologetics, but you are an expert in what Jesus has done in your life! You are an expert in how Jesus has set you free. When you give your testimony, focus on the mighty river of God's grace. When a cultist sees that you know you're a sinner who deserves to spend eternity apart from God, but you have absolute assurance that you are saved because of what Jesus has done for you, that will make an impact on the cultist.

KEEP THE FOLLOWING THINGS IN MIND WHEN GIVING YOUR TESTIMONY:

▶ **Describe what your life was like** before you were a Christian. What were your feelings, attitudes, actions, and relationships like during this time? (The apostle Paul clearly spoke of what his life was like before he was a Christian—Acts 26:4-11.)

▶ **What events transpired** in your life that led up to your decision to trust in Christ? What caused you to begin considering Christ as a solution to your needs? Be specific.

▶ **Describe your conversion experience.** Was it a book you read? Were you in a church? Were other Christians with you at the time? (Paul clearly spoke of how he became a Christian—Acts 26:12-18.)

▶ **What kind of change took place** in your life following your conversion? What effect did trusting in Christ have on your feelings, attitudes, actions, and relationships? (Paul spoke of how his life changed once becoming a Christian—Acts 26:19-23.)

▶ **Never forget that God works through people.** He uses people as instruments to reach out and bless other people; that's his chosen means. In the Old Testament God worked through Israel to bring blessing to others. The Jewish nation would be a light to the Gentiles, an instrument by which blessing would be communicated to all people everywhere. In the New Testament, the church is to be used as an instrument of God by which God reaches through his church to bring blessing to people around the world. Each one of us can be used as an instrument!

2 DON'T ASSUME EVERY CULTIST BELIEVES THE SAME THING

For example, individual Mormons often have different levels of knowledge:

- Some Mormons follow the rules so well that they're given a "recommend"—a pass that lets them enter the Mormon temple and learn secret things that less "worthy" members don't learn.

- Some Mormons are more knowledgeable because they pay attention to the messages given by the church's "living prophet," or study well before their two-year missionary service to represent the church, while others don't prepare as much.

So, don't tell a person what he or she believes. Instead, ask questions that end up in a constructive discussion that leads to an examination of biblical doctrine.

QUESTIONS TO OPEN A DISCUSSION:

GOD:
- Who do you believe God is?
- Do you believe there is only one true God?
- Do you believe in the Trinity: God in three persons: Father, Son, Holy Spirit?
- Do you believe God has always existed?

JESUS CHRIST:
- Who do you believe Jesus Christ is?
- Do you believe Jesus has always existed, or was he created?
- Do you believe Jesus is God? Is he equal to the Father in his divine nature?
- Do you believe Jesus earned his Godhood or has he always been God?
- Do you believe Jesus physically and bodily rose from the dead?

THE GOSPEL OF SALVATION:
- What do you believe a person has to do to be saved?
- Do you believe a person has to join your religion to be saved?
- Do you believe a person will lose salvation if that person leaves your religion?
- At what point do you know that you've done enough to be assured of eternal life?

9 EMPHASIZE THE GOSPEL

Cultists need to hear about God's grace more than anything else!

You can ask any cultist, "At what point in your religion do you know for sure that when you die you will be saved and accepted by God?" The cultist will not be able to give a definite answer, because his or her salvation is dependant upon performance.

For example, Mormons are told that they must prove themselves worthy to be accepted by God into the highest level of heaven. While many Mormons believe that they have all eternity to work toward perfection, most will readily admit that they are not far along in the process of achieving it. Also, many believe the statement in Mormon scripture that says, "Go your ways and sin no more; but unto that soul who sinneth shall the former sins return, saith the Lord your God" (Doctrine and Covenants 82:7). This is why a Mormon Church manual explains that, "Those who receive forgiveness and then repeat the sin are held accountable for their former sins" (Gospel Principles, 1978, 1992 ed., p. 253).

Mormons are under a heavy burden to constantly strive to confess and forsake their sins. Never can a Mormon say that he has full assurance that he is forgiven, because at any moment, he may repeat a sin that will make him "accountable" for his former sins.

This weight on the cultists' shoulders is unbearable. No one can survive this kind of legalism. How much better is the wonderful grace of God!

> "For it is by grace you have been saved, through faith—and this not from yourselves, it is the gift of God—not by works, so that no one can boast." —Ephesians 2:8–9
>
> "Though your sins are like scarlet, they shall be as white as snow; though they are red as crimson, they shall be like wool." —Isaiah 1:18
>
> "In [Jesus] we have redemption through his blood, the forgiveness of sins, in accordance with the riches of God's grace." —Ephesians 1:7
>
> "Their sins and lawless acts I will remember no more." —Hebrews 10:17
>
> "Blessed is he whose transgressions are forgiven, whose sins are covered." —Psalm 32:1

3. CULTISTS ARE TRAINED TO ANSWER OBJECTIONS

Many who have talked with Jehovah's Witnesses and Mormons would say that they seem to have an answer for everything.

The reason they seem to have answers for every question is because they've been carefully trained, and often have months—or years—of practice. For example, active Jehovah's Witnesses not only go door-to-door responding to householders' objections, but they have weekly training sessions where they learn what to say to someone like you.

So, what is the solution? Simply move the discussion back to the Bible. Don't worry if they are giving you rote responses that they have memorized. Just keep presenting evidence that their leaders are not telling them the truth and keep taking them back to the Bible. Eventually, the rote responses will stop.

One helpful technique is to request that they read a particular verse aloud, and then ask: "What is being said here?" If they repeat the typical cultic interpretation, ask them to read it aloud again, slowly and carefully—and follow it with another question. If you are persistent, you'll help them see for themselves the contradictions and problems with their view.

Note also that cultists are trained how to respond to common comebacks. For example, they are taught how to respond if people say: "I'm not interested," "I have my own religion," "We are already Christians here," "I'm busy," "Why do you people call so often?," "I am already well acquainted with your work," or "We have no money." When someone raises such an objection, this automatically triggers a response in the mind of the cultist. Keeping this fact in mind will help you to remain patient with the cultist.

8 DEMONSTRATE JESUS' DEITY

Cultists always get the identity of Jesus wrong.

To witness effectively to cultists, you will need to be prepared to show the cultist that Jesus is the eternal God. Here's one way to do this: Compare the Old Testament descriptions and attributes of God with the New Testament descriptions and attributes of Jesus Christ.

Descriptions and Attributes	God in the Old Testament	Jesus in the New Testament
Creator	Isaiah 44:24	Colossians 1:16; John 1:3
Savior	Isaiah 43:11	Titus 2:13–14; Jude 4
Shepherd	Psalm 23:1-2	John 10:11-18
Great Judge	Psalm 98:9	John 5:21-22
First and Last	Isaiah 44:6; 48:12	Revelation 1:17-18
Holy One	Isaiah 47:4	Acts 3:14; John 6:69
Glory	Isaiah 6:1–5	John 12:41
Omnipotent (all-powerful)	Jeremiah 32:17, 27	Matthew 19:26
Omniscient (all-knowing)	Psalm 147:5	1 John 3:20
Omnipresent (present everywhere)	Jeremiah 23:24	Matthew 28:20
Gives Eternal Life	Deuteronomy 30:20	Romans 6:23

With these verses, the cultist will likely go home with a different view of Jesus. If that happens, God the Holy Spirit will be working on his or her heart, convicting and bringing to mind the things of Jesus Christ.

CHRISTIAN RESPONSES TO OBJECTIONS COMMONLY RAISED BY CULTISTS

The word "Trinity" is not found in the Bible and is therefore not a biblical idea. Just because a word is not found in the Bible, doesn't mean that it is not a biblical concept. For example, the word "theocracy" (God-ruled nation) is not in the Bible, yet Israel was a theocracy. In the same way, the Trinity concept is seen throughout Scripture.

The Trinity is confusing, so God would not exist as a Trinity. Finite humans cannot fully comprehend God, who is infinite (Isaiah 55:8).

Jesus is God's Son and is "with" God, so he cannot be God himself. Jesus is the second person of the Trinity, distinct from — and yet equal in nature to—the Father (Jn. 1:1; Col. 2:9). As God's "Son," he possesses God's full nature (Jn. 5:18; 19:7; Lev. 24:16).

Jesus said the Father is greater than him, so he cannot be "equal" to God (John 14:28). In his human nature, the Father was "greater" than Jesus, but in his God nature, Jesus is equal to the Father (Jn. 5:18).

Since God is invisible and cannot die, Jesus cannot be God. Jesus' is the visible "image" of the invisible God (Jn. 1:18; 14:9; Heb. 1:3; 2 Cor. 4:4). He died in his humanity, but in his deity, he remained alive (Phil. 2:5-11; Jn. 2:18-22).

4 CHECK SCRIPTURES

When cultists quote a verse it is typically out of context.

Never take the cultist's interpretation of a passage at face value because they often misinterpret the passage to suit their own agenda.

For example, the Bahá'ís claim that their prophet Bahá'u'lláh was prophesied by Jesus in John 14:16. In that passage, Jesus talked about "another Counselor," and the Bahá'í cult says that Jesus was referring to Bahá'u'lláh who would come in the nineteenth century. But the Bahá'ís completely distort the teachings of Jesus, because Jesus identifies the Counselor as the Holy Spirit in verse 26. Jesus said that the Holy Spirit would come in a few days (Acts 1:5), not in the nineteenth century. Jesus said that the Holy Spirit would be with us forever, but Bahá'u'lláh died after a few decades. Also, Jesus said that the Holy Spirit would remind us of everything he had taught, not that he would teach entirely different doctrines from an entirely different prophet. Going to the verse and looking it up in context dispels the mythological interpretation imposed upon it by the cult.

Another example is the Jehovah's Witnesses' claim that the Bible condemns birthdays in Matthew 14:6-10, because it says that on Herod's birthday, he had John the Baptist executed. However, this passage proves only that Herod was evil, not that birthdays are evil. One will search this passage and other passages in vain to find a single statement where God explicitly condemns birthday celebrations.

Remember these things when interpreting Scripture:

Always examine the context of the verse quoted by cultists. Ask: Who is speaking in this passage? What is the setting? Who is being addressed? What is the main point of the passage? Look to the context for answers to these questions.

Interpreting Scripture is about drawing the meaning out of the Bible verses, not putting a meaning onto the verses. Ask the cultist: Where does this passage clearly teach what you are claiming?

If a verse is unclear, examine it in light of clear passages. Bible verses are not disconnected fragments, but are embedded in the whole of Scripture. Ask: What does the Bible clearly teach in other places? How does the overall teaching in the Bible on this subject help us understand what this particular verse means?

6 ASK STRATEGIC QUESTIONS

You can't force good doctrine on a person trapped in a cult; instead, ask questions that cause him or her to think critically.

Examples of Strategic Questions for Mormons:

▶ If you're talking with a Mormon who thinks that human beings can become gods, ask: How do you interpret Isaiah 43:10, which reads, "Before me no god was formed, nor will there be one after me"?

▶ If the Bible has many mistakes, as Mormons claim, why does the Mormon church continue to publish and distribute the King James Version to church members?

▶ I noticed Mormon churches do not display the cross. Since Paul gloried "in the cross" of Christ (Galatians 6:14), why don't Mormons glory in it as well? Do you believe the atonement took place on the cross or in the garden of Gethsemane? If the Mormon answers that most of the atonement took place in the garden, ask: Why did Jesus have to die on the cross if his suffering in the garden atoned for the majority of our sins?

▶ If the Mormon asks you to pray about the Book of Mormon, ask: Which Book of Mormon do you want me to pray about? The 1830 edition? The 1921 edition? Or today's edition, which has over 4,000 changes from the original 1830 edition?

Examples of Strategic Questions for Jehovah's Witnesses:

▶ If the Jehovah's Witnesses are the only true witnesses for God, and if the Jehovah's Witnesses as an organization came into being in the late nineteenth century (which is a historical fact), does this mean God was without a witness for over eighteen centuries throughout church history?

▶ If Jesus is Michael the Archangel, why was Jesus able to rebuke Satan at Matthew 16:23 when Michael didn't have the authority to rebuke Satan at Jude 9?

▶ According to Acts 1:8, 2:32, 3:15, 4:33, and 13:30-31, were the early Christians witnesses of Jehovah or witnesses of Jesus Christ?

▶ If there is no other Savior than God (Isaiah 43:11), then doesn't this mean that New Testament references to Jesus as Savior point to his deity (Titus 2:13)?

TALKING WITH EX-CULTISTS

DO let the ex-cultist know he or she is not alone. Help the person find a Christian support group of ex-members (many are on the Internet at www.meetup.com), and give the person ex-member testimonies to read. (For example, see the testimonies at www.4mormon.org and www.4jehovah.org.)

DO NOT pressure the ex-cultist into church attendance or Christian activities too soon. Remember that in the cult, meeting attendance was likely mandatory; so a simple, "I missed you at church last night; where were you?" question from a well-meaning Christian can scare off an ex-cultist.

DO demonstrate the love of Christ by unconditionally accepting the ex-cultist regardless of his or her issues with Christianity. Remember that in the cult, it was not acceptable to act or believe differently, so be sensitive to the ex-cultist's insecurity about the commitment level of your friendship.

DO create a "safe" environment for the ex-cultist to ask his or her questions. Never belittle the person's ideas or questions or put them down by saying, "I would never believe …" or "I would never do …"

DO help the ex-cultist feel accepted and normal. Remember that ex-cultists already feel inferior because of their prior involvement in a cult, and most would not have joined the cult if they had known all the facts.

DO NOT tell the ex-cultist WHAT to think, but HOW to think. Remember that in the cult, members were not allowed to think for themselves; so the ex-cultist will need to learn how to research and find answers to the questions they have about God, the Bible, and Christianity.

DO point the ex-cultist to a relationship with Jesus. Ex-cultists are hungry for something to believe in and belong to. As a result, people often leave one cult only to join another. Instead of pointing them to your church or another religious association, you must point them to Jesus. Emphasize that he is the only one who can fulfill the deepest longings of the human heart.

© 2008 Bristol Works, Inc.
Rose Publishing, Inc.
4733 Torrance Blvd., #259
Torrance, CA 90503 U.S.A.
email: info@rose-publishing.com
www.rose-publishing.com

Rose Publishing has more than 100 Bible reference pamphlets.

All rights reserved. It is illegal to copy, transmit electronically, or reproduce this pamphlet in whole or in part in any form. Printed in the USA. May not be posted or transmitted on the internet.   060914SCG

Principal Author: Ron Rhodes, ThD, President, Reasoning from the Scriptures Ministries
Co-Author: Christy (Harvey) Darlington, President, Witnesses for Jesus, Inc.

Other products available from Rose Publishing:
10 Q & A Jehovah's Witnesses pamphlet and PowerPoint®
10 Q & A Mormonism pamphlet and PowerPoint®
Christianity, Cults & Religions pamphlet, chart, and PowerPoint®

All Scripture quotations, unless otherwise indicated, are taken from the Holy Bible, New International Version®. NIV®. Copyright © 1973, 1978, 1984 by International Bible Society. Used by permission of Zondervan. All rights reserved.

ISBN-13: 978-159636-198-0
ISBN-10: 159636-198-0

Stock #658X *10 Keys to Witnessing to Cults* pamphlet
Retailers: Package of 5 pamphlets = Stock #659X (ISBN-13: 978-159636-199-7)

7 BE LOVING

It's not just what you say, it's how you say it!

Sharing your faith isn't just about strong answers from the Bible; it's about being sold out to Jesus Christ. If a person knows all the right answers but is arrogant, prideful, and has an "in your face" attitude, this isn't the kind of person who is going to draw people to the real Jesus.

So, unless the situation calls for it, try to avoid a highly confrontational approach. For example, you could say to a Mormon: "My friend, you worship a false god proclaimed by a false prophet and a false book called the Book of Mormon and a false gospel based upon works." And you'd be technically correct! But that approach may turn the Mormon off to the true message you are trying to communicate. You may win the argument, but lose the Mormon.

Consider a gentler approach in which you say, "My friend, I really care about you, and I'm afraid you might get deceived into believing a lie. I'm afraid you might die and go into eternity believing something that isn't true. Can we talk about this? Can I share with you why I believe the Bible is true?" Focus on keeping a loving attitude in your heart.

Let your love be genuine and embracing. People can sense if you truly care about them, as opposed to merely acting like you care only because you want to convert them. Pray that the Holy Spirit would fill your heart with love that shows itself in meaningful ways to your cultic acquaintances. This kind of love is sacrificial and self-giving, and involves showing hospitality to people (Ephesians 5:2; 1 Timothy 4:12; 1 Corinthians 16:14).

You'll be amazed at what God will do through a person who is sold out to Jesus Christ, allowing Jesus' grace and love to flow through him or her when approaching someone in a cult. Strong answers from that kind of person mean a lot. Let Jesus' love shine through you!

If the cultist becomes a Christian, the love has to continue. There's a good chance that his cult will expel him, and nearly everyone in his life will shun him. He may also lose his family, so he will need to be brought into a new family. As his new brothers and sisters in Christ, you must make sure that he feels at home in his new church and that discipleship is an ongoing priority. Part of being loving means that you don't drop the ball at conversion but help him to become a true, lifelong disciple of Christ.

5 DEFINE TERMS

There is a communication block between the cultist and the Christian that can be removed by defining key Christian words and ideas.

Consider, for example, this phrase: "Jesus Christ is the Son of God. He died for the sins of mankind, and then resurrected from the dead. Scripture speaks of his second coming." Jehovah's Witnesses, Mormons, and many other cults would all agree with this statement, but they would interpret it differently from the traditional Christian view.

Jehovah's Witnesses will say:

- "Yes, Jesus is the Christ"—but they would argue that Jesus was not the "Christ" at his birth, but became the "Christ" at his baptism.

- "Yes, Jesus is the Son of God"—but they view the term "Son of God" as a lesser "god" than God the Father because they claim Jesus was created by God.

- "Yes, Jesus died for the sins of mankind"—but they would say that his blood covers one's sin only if one proves oneself worthy through door-to-door activity.

- "Yes, Jesus was resurrected"—but they will say it was not a physical resurrection. Instead, he was resurrected spiritually as Michael the Archangel.

- "Yes, Scripture speaks of his second coming"—but they claim that this prophecy is already in the process of being fulfilled through an "invisible presence" of Christ in 1914.

Mormons will say:

- "Yes, Jesus is the Christ"—but they would add that Jesus had to compete with Lucifer over who would be the savior of the world.

- "Yes, Jesus is the Son of God"—but they would say that he is the "Son" only because he was born in heaven as a spirit baby to God the Father and one of his spirit wives.

- "Yes, Jesus died for the sins of mankind"—but they would claim that the majority of his atonement took place in the Garden of Gethsemane, rather than on the cross.

- "Yes, Jesus' blood covers the sins of mankind"—but they would add works as a requirement for entrance into the highest level of heaven.

Mormons, Jehovah's Witnesses, and other cults mean something entirely different by their use of these traditional Christian terms. Never assume you are communicating clearly in a conversation unless you have taken the time to define your terms biblically.